D1799673

A is for Alligator

Nancy J. Bringhurst

A is for **A**lligator

written by
Nancy J. Bringhurst

illustrated by
Mindy C. Stark

OBERLIN PRESS

Ashland, Oregon

Published by
OBERLIN PRESS
A division of Wellstone Press
9870 Mt. Ashland Ski Road
Ashland, Oregon 97520

First printing August 2001
10 9 8 7 6 5 4 3 2 1

ISBN 1-93085-01-9

PRINTED IN KOREA

For Danny, Ashley, Michael,
Hannah, Gregory, and Willie
N.J.B.

For my Little Mama, my Padre, and for Bear
M.C.S.

A is for **Alligator** trying on a new shoe.

Should she get red?
Purple? Or blue?

B is for **Bear** with a bad tummy ache.

Now why would a bear eat chocolate cake?

C is for Crocodile

climbing a tree.

That looks pretty silly,
don't you agree?

D is for **Duck** who's just caught a whale.

Do you think it will fit
in the fishing pail?

E is for Elephant whose trunk is too long.

How did that happen?
What went wrong?

F is for Frog who's riding a pig.

But why do you think
she's wearing a wig?

G is for **Giraffe** tucked snug in his bed.

Now where in the world will he put his head?

H is for **Hamster** who ate the whole pie.

Could that be what made the baker cry?

I is for Insect with long curly hair.

Don't you think that's very rare?

J is for Jaguar who just lost a race.

What a poor sport!
Just look at his face.

K is for **Kangaroo** with an extra pouch.

How will she ever sit down on the couch?

L is for **Lion** having her toenails painted.

Why do you think that poor lady fainted?

M is for Monkey who plays the guitar.

Have you ever seen anything quite so bizarre?

N is for **Newt** in a pink flowered skirt.

Can you help her choose the prettiest shirt?

O is for Octopus eating his snack.

Did all that come out of his tiny backpack?

P is for Porcupine who just wants to play.

So why does everyone run away?

Q is for **Quail** who built a square boat.

But the question is — will it ever float?

R is for Racoon who loves to ski.

Uh oh!

Is he going to hit that tree?

S is for Snail in the coffee cup.

Is that why that lady might throw up?

T is for Turkey who won't eat his dinner.

Now, why do you think he wants to get thinner?

U is for **Unicorn** on the pitcher's mound.

Have you ever seen a unicorn on your playground?

V is for **Vulture**
watching TV.

But sometimes the story is much
too scary.

W is for **Worms** who like to ride, too.

But no one will sit with them, would you?

X is for **X-Ray** that sees through the skin.

Do you think that would work on a dolphin's fin?

Y is for Yak in the barbershop.

How will the barber know
when to stop?

Z is for Zebra with ears to the floor.

What happens if they get caught in the door?